Circus

Circus 123

Denise M. Jordan

Heinemann Library

Chicago, Illinois

Designed by Sue Emerson, Heinemann Library
Printed and bound in the U.S.A. by Lake Book

06 05
10 9 8 7 6 5 4 3 2

Library of Congress Cataloging-in-Publication Data
Jordan, Denise M.
   Circus 1, 2, 3 / Denise Jordan.
      p. cm. — (Circus)
Includes index.
Summary: A counting book featuring the people and animals of the circus.
   ISBN: 1-58810-545-8 (HC), 1-58810-753-1 (Pbk.)
   1. Circus—Juvenile literature. 2. Counting—Juvenile literature. [1.
   Circus. 2. Counting.] I. Title: Circus one, two, three. II. Title.
      GV1817 .J67 2002
      793.3—dc21

                                2001004793

Acknowledgments
The author and publishers are grateful to the following for permission to reproduce copyright material:
pp. 3, 22 Greg Williams/Heinemann Library; p. 5 Jane Faircloth/Transparencies, Inc.; p. 7 Robert Cavin/Transparencies, Inc.; p. 9 B. Seed/Trip; p. 11 E. R. Degginger/Color Pic, Inc.; p. 13 Ottmar Bierwagen/spectrumstock.com; p. 15 John Coletti/Stock, Boston Inc./PictureQuest; p. 17 Jacques Charlas/Stock, Boston Inc./PictureQuest; p. 19 S. Grant/Trip; p. 21 Dean Conger/Corbis; p. 23 glossary (animal trainer) Louisa Preston

Cover photographs courtesy of (L-R): Greg Williams/Heinemann Library; John Coletti/Stock, Boston Inc./PictureQuest; Jacques Charlas/Stock, Boston Inc./PictureQuest

Every effort has been made to contact copyright holders of any material reproduced in this book. Any omissions will be rectified in subsequent printings if notice is given to the publisher.

Special thanks to our advisory panel for their help in the preparation of this book:

Eileen Day, Preschool Teacher
Chicago, IL

Paula Fischer, K–1 Teacher
Indianapolis, IN

Sandra Gilbert,
Library Media Specialist
Houston, TX

Angela Leeper,
Educational Consultant
North Carolina Department
of Public Instruction
Raleigh, NC

Pam McDonald, Reading Teacher
Winter Springs, FL

Melinda Murphy,
Library Media Specialist
Houston, TX

Helen Rosenberg, MLS
Chicago, IL

Anna Marie Varakin,
Reading Instructor
Western Maryland College

The publishers would also like to thank Fred Dahlinger, Jr., Director of Collections and Research at the Circus World Museum in Baraboo, Wisconsin, and Smita Parida for their help in reviewing the contents of this book.

Some words are shown in bold, **like this.**
You can find them in the picture glossary on page 23.

One 1

The circus is about to start.

How many **ringmasters** do you see?

Two 2

Some **acrobats** can bend their bodies.

How many acrobats do you see?

Three   3

There are **rings** under
the big top.

How many rings
do you see?

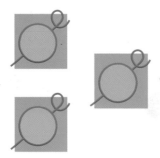

Four 4

Chimpanzees play in a band.

How many chimpanzees do you see?

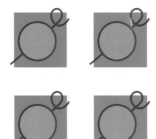

Five 5

Elephants can do tricks.

How many elephants
do you see?

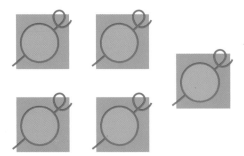

Six   6

Children like to watch
the circus.

How many children
do you see?

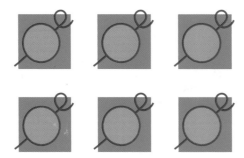

Seven   7

Acrobats are very strong.

How many acrobats
do you see?

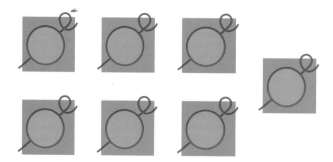

Eight 8

Tigers snarl and roar
at the **animal trainer**.

How many tigers
do you see?

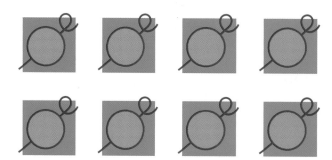

Nine 9

Circus dogs exercise
in the yard.

How many dogs
do you see?

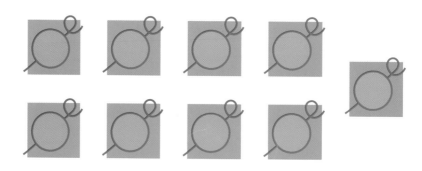

Ten　10

Circus horses bow
and dance.

How many horses
do you see?

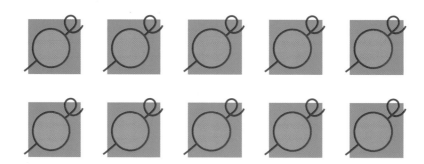

One **ringmaster** says goodbye.

Come again next year.

Picture Glossary

acrobat
pages 4–5, 14–15

ring
pages 6–7

animal trainer
pages 16–17

ringmaster
pages 3, 22

chimpanzee
pages 8–9

Note to Parents and Teachers

Using this book, children can practice basic mathematical skills while learning interesting facts about the circus. Help children see the relationship between the numerals 1 through 10 and the block icons at the bottom of each text page. Extend the concept by drawing ten "blocks" on a sheet of construction paper. Cut out the paper "blocks." Together, read *Circus 123*, and as you do so, ask the child to place the appropriate number of "blocks" on the photograph. This activity can also be done using manipulatives such as dried beans or small plastic beads.

Index